[PIC]TURING THE PAST

Mesopotamia

Iraq in Ancient Times

PETER CHRISP

ENCHANTED LION BOOKS
New York

First American Edition published in 2004 by Enchanted Lion Books, 115 West 18 Street, New York, NY 10011

Library of Congress Cataloging-in-Publication Data
Chrisp, Peter.
Mesopotamia, Iraq in ancient times / by Peter Chrisp.
p.cm.— (Picturing the past)
Includes bibliographical references (p.) and index.
ISBN 1-59270-024-1
1. Iraq—Civilization—To 634—Juvenile literature. [1. Iraq—Civilization—To 634.] I. Title. II. Series.
DS71.C48 2004
935—dc22 2003071032

Produced for Enchanted Lion Books by Arcturus Publishing Ltd, 26/27 Bickels Yard, 151-153 Bermondsey Street, London SE1 3HA.

Series concept: Alex Woolf
Editors: Liz Gogerly, Margot Richardson
Designer: Simon Borrough
Picture researcher: Shelley Noronha, Glass Onion Pictures

Printed and bound in Italy.

Titles in the series: Picturing the Past
Ancient Egypt
Ancient Greece
Mesopotamia: Iraq in Ancient Times
Ancient Rome

Picture Acknowledgements:
AKG-images (Erich Lessing) 26; Ancient Art and Architecture Collection Ltd 20; The Art Archive 7, 8, 9, 10, 11, 17 19, 21, 22, 23, 25, 27; Bridgeman Art Library/www.bridgman.co.uk (Ashmolean Museum, Oxford) 14, 16; The British Museum 15, Corbis 5; University of Pennsylvania Museum (neg S8-22100) 13.

All artwork by Peter bull Art Studio, including cover and title page.

Front cover: The Art Archive
Back cover:
Bronze head (inside book, p10): The Art Archive/ Archaeological Museum Baghdad/ Dagli Orti
Rounded Tablet with cuneiform writing (inside book, p8): The Art Archive/ Musee du Louvre Paris/ Dagli Orti
Relief carving (inside book, page 27): The Art Archive/ British Museum/ Dagli Orti

Note to parents and teachers
Every effort has been made by the publishers to ensure that these websites are suitable for children; that they are of the highest educational value; and that they contain no inappropriate or offensive material. However, because of the nature of the Internet, it is impossible to guarantee that the contents of these sites will not be altered. We strongly advise that Internet access is supervised by a responsible adult.

Contents

The First Cities

Mesopotamia is a Greek word, meaning "the land between the rivers." These rivers are the Tigris and the Euphrates, which wind their way south from the mountains of what is now eastern Turkey, and across the flat plains of present-day Iraq, until they pour into the Persian Gulf.

WEBLINK
http://www.mesopotamia.co.uk

A good general site on Mesopotamian civilization, from the British Museum.

Mesopotamia is part of the "fertile crescent," a curve of land stretching from the Persian Gulf north and west to the Mediterranean Sea. It was here, more than ten thousand years ago, that people, for the first time ever, learned to produce their food by farming. Instead of moving from place to place, hunting animals and gathering wild plant foods, they settled down, growing crops and keeping sheep and cattle. In one part of the fertile crescent, Mesopotamia, villages grew into towns and then cities, the first in the world. It was in these cities that writing, kingship, temples, irrigation, bronze-making, written laws, and many other features of later civilizations were invented.

MESOPOTAMIA
This map shows the major cities of the Mesopotamian civilization, as well as the Tigris and Euphrates rivers, which have shifted their courses many times throughout history.

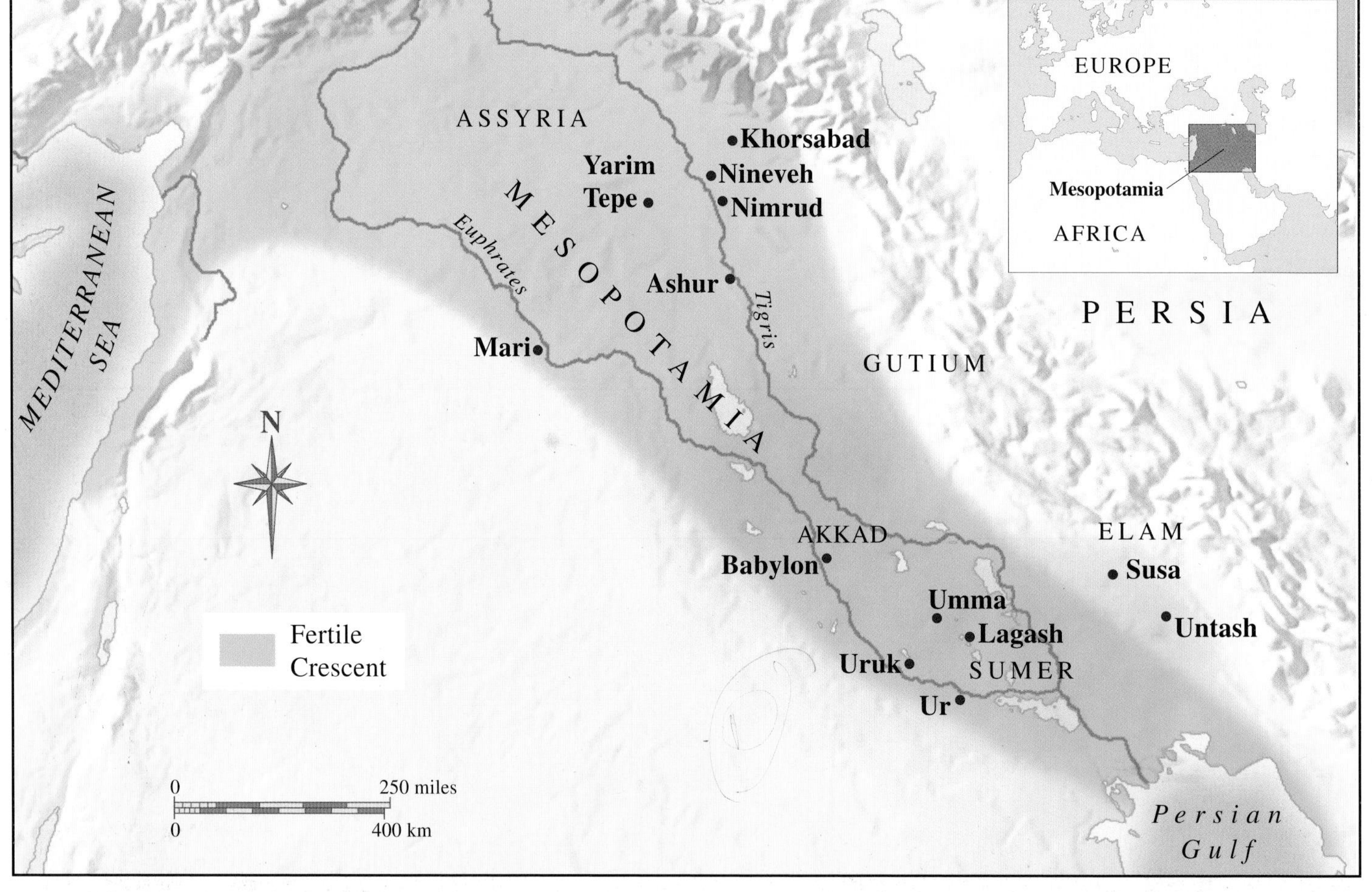

HOW DO WE KNOW?

For thousands of years, early Mesopotamian history was forgotten. The only signs that the civilization had ever existed were large earth mounds, called tells, which stood out against the plains. Tells were formed over thousands of years, from fallen buildings made of dried mud bricks and other rubbish left behind by ancient people. From the early nineteenth century, European travellers began to dig into the tells. They found the ruins of ancient palaces and temples, together with sculpture, pottery and other treasures. They had rediscovered the world's first cities.

Over time, many different peoples speaking different languages lived in the Mesopotamian area.

The civilization was created around 4000BCE by people who lived in a region called Sumer, in southern Mesopotamia. These people were the Sumerians, who built the first cities, such as Ur and Uruk. Around 2350BCE, Sumer was conquered by Sargon, king of Akkad, the region to the north, who created the world's first empire. Akkadian, a language related to Arabic and Hebrew, replaced Sumerian as the main language. Yet despite changes of language, the arrival of new peoples, and the rise and fall of more empires, the main features of Mesopotamian civilization, such as the writing system, continued for thousands of years.

URUK

These mounds are the remains of a great brick ziggurat, or temple tower, at Uruk, the first important Mesopotamian city. You can see how the ruins stand out against the flat desert of southern Iraq.

Irrigation and Farming

Like Egypt, where another early civilization developed, the region of Mesopotamia, where Iraq is today, is a hot climate with little rain. In both ancient civilizations, it was only possible to grow food thanks to the annual flooding of rivers – the Nile in Egypt and the Tigris and the Euphrates in Mesopotamia. Unlike the Nile, which flooded at the right time of year to plant crops, Mesopotamia's rivers flooded when the crops were already growing in the fields. The water had to be channeled and stored, so that later it could be used to water the fields.

In early times, people lived and farmed close to the rivers. To prevent floods from washing away their villages, they built dykes, raised mounds on the river banks. They dug canals and ditches to carry the water away from the river to reservoirs. Canals also carried water to areas which had previously been desert, allowing more and more food to be produced.

The rivers also carried silt, which was left behind after the flood season ended. To prevent the canals filling up, this silt

WEBLINK

http://teamwork.ucdavis.edu/~gel115/115CH17oldirrigation.html

Find out about irrigation in Mesopotamia and other ancient societies.

Canal Repair
These men are cleaning the silt out of an irrigation canal, using copper-bladed shovels and baskets made of reeds. They receive their orders from a local official called a *gugallum*, or canal inspector.

had to be dug out regularly. This was hard work, but everyone knew that it had to be done to stop the land returning to desert.

The most important food crops were barley and dates. Date palm trees are either male or female. Male flowers produce pollen, which female flowers use to make fruit. One male tree produces enough pollen for fifty female trees. To have plenty of dates, Mesopotamian farmers grew more female trees, cutting down most male trees for wood. Usually pollen is carried from tree to tree by insects, such as bees. With so few male trees, farmers did this job themselves.

Growing Dates
To pollinate the date trees by hand, Mesopotamian farmers climbed ladders to put pollen from the male flowers onto the female flowers.

Large Farms
Mesopotamian rulers owned great farming estates, such as the one shown on this carving, dating from around 700BCE. Houses and other buildings are in the center, with palm trees at the bottom.

HOW DO WE KNOW?

The number and size of ruined Mesopotamian cities, in areas which are now desert, show that irrigation and farming were carried out on a massive scale. How else could the people who lived in these cities be fed? We also have the evidence of thousands of dried up ancient irrigation canals, found across the deserts of southern Iraq. More evidence comes from ancient texts concerning farming, including instructions for irrigating fields and planting and harvesting crops.

Writing

The Sumerians needed to keep records of cattle, sheep and crops. Around 3300BCE, they began to do this by drawing simple pictures on clay tablets. A picture of a bull's head was used to show cattle, while an ear of barley stood for grain. Pictures could also be used to show ideas. A drawing of a foot, for example, could stand for a journey. Over time, the style of drawing changed, with curved lines becoming groups of straight wedges, the quickest marks to make with a cut reed called a stylus. From these marks, Mesopotamian writing was called "cuneiform," meaning wedge-shaped

By 3100BCE, people had realized that a sign could be used to show the sound of the word as well as the object itself. So the sign for a bull could be the sound "gu" (bull in Sumerian), while the sign for a fish could be "ku" (fish in Sumerian). By grouping sound signs together, people could now spell different words. In doing this, they had invented writing.

TABLET

Many thousands of clay tablets with cuneiform writing have been found, including whole libraries, often baked hard in ancient fires. This tablet has a list of different goods. Numbers were made by pushing the blunt end of the stylus into the clay, making circles and crescents. This is an early form of cuneiform, with signs still resembling pictures.

SCRIBE

A scribe writes on a soft clay tablet, using a reed stylus. Around his neck, he has a "cylinder seal," which he can roll onto the clay to leave his signature. Cylinder seals were made from metal, stone, bone and shell.

HOW DO WE KNOW?

The fact that we can read cuneiform today is largely thanks to an English scholar named Henry Rawlinson. In 1825, he found long cuneiform inscriptions carved on a high cliff face in Iran, in three ancient languages: Babylonian, Elamite and Old Persian. Rawlinson copied these, and correctly guessed that the signs at the start of each text were the name of the Persian king, Darius. By trial and error, he went on to read more and more of the signs. First he deciphered the Old Persian inscription, using his knowledge of the modern form of the language. He then spent years deciphering the other two languages.

SEAL
Cylinder seals were used to sign letters and to seal jars or doors to protect valuables. This plaster impression, made by the seal on the right, shows the scribe, who is the figure on the left, being presented to a seated goddess by another goddess.

WEBLINK
http://www.mesopotamia.co.uk/writing/explore/exp_main.html

Find out about the work of Mesopotamian scribes.

Cuneiform was a difficult writing system to learn. While our alphabet has just twenty-six letters, there were more than six hundred cuneiform signs. Some boys were sent to school at a young age to train to be professional writers, called scribes, but only wealthy people could afford to have their sons trained. We know about school lessons thanks to thousands of exercise tablets that have been found. These have a text written by a teacher on one side, with a pupil's copy, less skilfully done, on the other. Some of these exercises describe schoolboys' lives: "When I rose early in the morning, I faced my mother and said to her, 'Give me my lunch, I want to go to school!' My mother gave me two rolls and I set out."

Although cuneiform was invented for record keeping, many more uses were found for it. It was used to write down laws, histories, stories, hymns, letters, scientific texts, magic spells and recipes. It continued to be used for almost 3,200 years, by many different peoples across western Asia.

Craftworkers

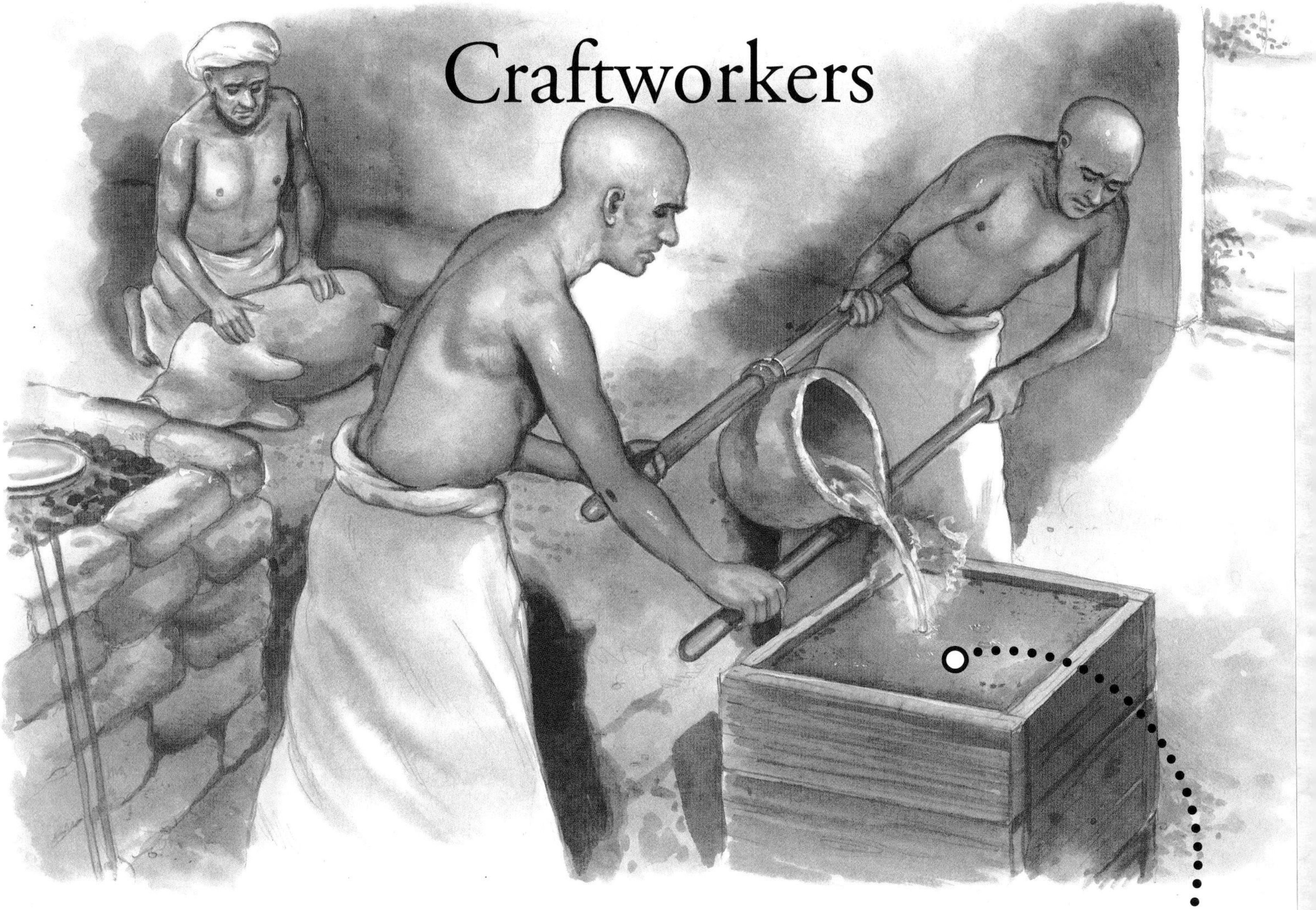

WORKSHOP
The man on the left is using skin bellows to pump air into a furnace, to make it hotter until the copper can be melted. On the right, two men pour molten copper into a mould, to make a statue.

KING'S HEAD
This head of a king, dating from 2300-2200BCE, was made from copper. It once had eyes, probably made from precious stones.

The Mesopotamians were experts at making tools, weapons and sculptures out of metal. At first, the main metal they used was copper. Then some time before 3000BCE, they discovered that adding a small amount of tin to the copper made a new harder metal, called bronze. Bronze was much better for making tools and weapons. It also melted at a lower temperature than copper, was more fluid, and was easier to cast.

To make flat tools, such as knives, the craftworkers carved their shape on a

WEBLINK
http://www.unc.edu/courses/rometech/public/content/arts_and_crafts/Sara_Malone/BRONZE_3.html

Find out about ancient bronze casting.

flat stone. Then they heated lumps of copper and tin together in a stone or pottery vessel, called a crucible, until they melted. The liquid bronze was then poured into the stone mould.

To make statues and bowls, the Mesopotamians invented a method called the "lost wax" process. First they made a model out of wax, or of clay covered with wax. Clay was packed around the model to make a mould. This was heated, so that the wax melted and drained out through holes. Liquid metal was poured into the mould, filling the space left by the "lost wax." Once the metal had cooled and hardened, the clay mould was broken open to reveal the sculpture.

Mesopotamians were also fine potters. Some time before 4500BCE, they invented the potter's wheel, which allowed them to shape a bowl while turning it. The earliest pots were made on a slow wheel. Around 2000BCE, they invented a fast-turning wheel, which allowed them to make vessels with thinner walls in a quicker time.

Pot of Tools
In about 2500BCE, someone in the city of Susa, capital of Elam, buried this collection of bronze tools and other items in a pottery jar, probably for safe keeping. From the jar's shape, we can tell that it was made on a slow-turning wheel. A fast wheel would make a more regular shape.

HOW DO WE KNOW?

In any ancient site, the commonest craft item found is pottery. Unlike metal objects, which can be melted and recycled, a broken pot can only be thrown away. While wood or textiles decay, pottery will last for ever in the earth. Metal objects, such as the copper head of the king, survive more rarely. Evidence for how they were made comes from examining the objects themselves. Archaeologists have found stone moulds used to make knives, still scorched black by hot metal. The "lost wax" method was also invented in other countries, such as China and East Africa, and is still used today.

Trade

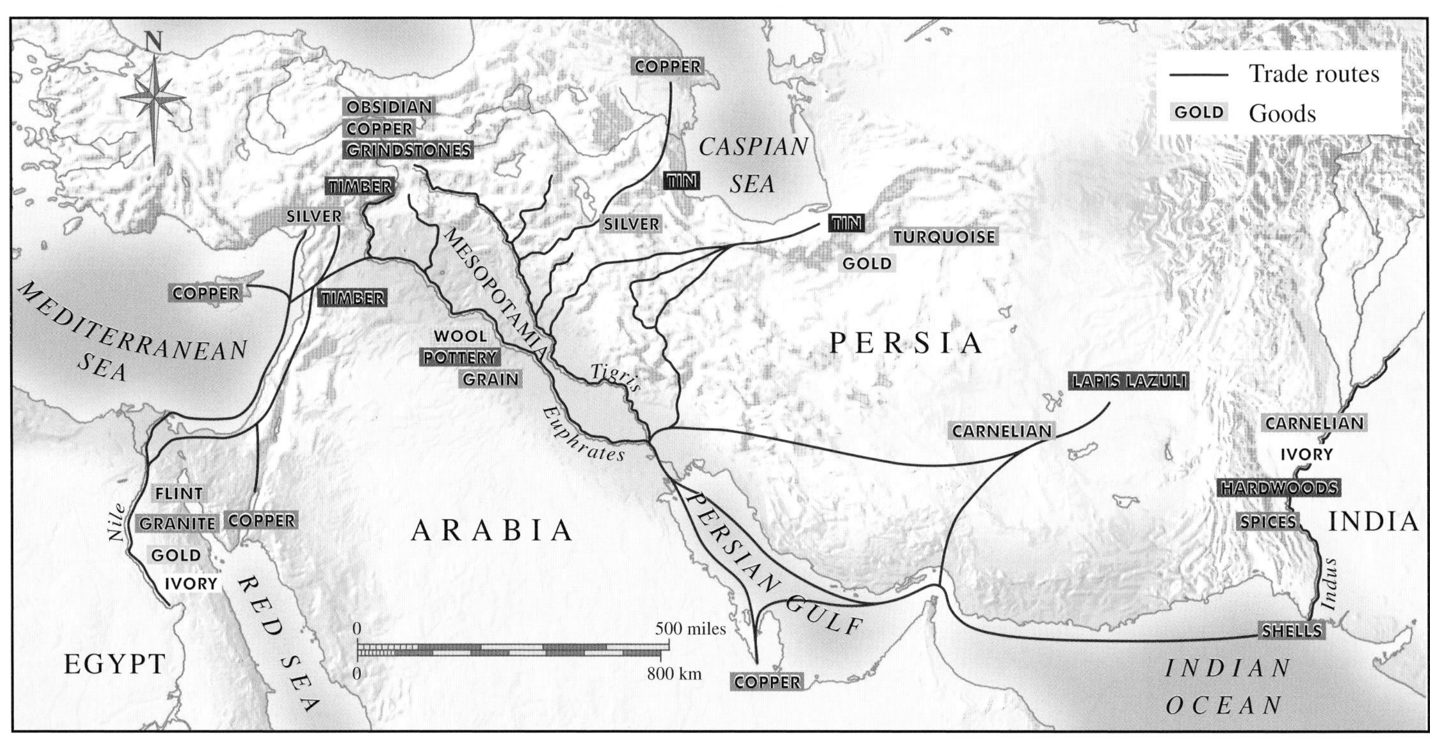

WEBLINK
http://www.mesopotamia.co.uk/trade/home_set.html

The British Museum's site on trade and transport.

Mesopotamia had plenty of clay, bitumen (natural tar), reeds and palm trees, whose wood is only good for making rough beams. The country lacked all other raw materials, such as stone, metal, and good timber for building or making furniture. So from the beginnings of Mesopotamian civilization, people had to trade with other lands to get the materials they needed.

The easiest way to transport heavy goods, such as stones, was by water, along rivers and canals and across the sea. Boats were made of bundles of reeds, waterproofed by coating them with bitumen. Reed boats are still used in Iraq today, and remains of ancient boats show that they have been built in the same way for at least 7,500 years.

It was much easier to row a boat downstream, carried along by the current, than upstream. For journeys upriver, donkeys were often used to pull the boats. They could also carry goods across land, where no water route existed.

Large amounts of tin and copper were imported to make bronze. Bronze items, such as tools and weapons, were then sold abroad. Other goods sold abroad included textiles, pottery, barley and dates. Grindstones, which every family needed for grinding barley into flour, were imported in vast quantities from the north. At a place now called Yarim Tepe, archaeologists found a building, dating from 4500BCE, in which a single room held several hundred grindstones. This must have been a merchant's warehouse.

There was long-distance trade with another ancient civilization, the Indus people of northern India, who sold precious stones, such as carnelian. Indian carnelian was used in Mesopotamian jewellery and works of art.

HOW DO WE KNOW?

Objects in Mesopotamian sites made of stone or metal, like the silver boat below, must have been made of materials from other lands. This is evidence of long distance trade. Seals used by Indian merchants have also been found in Mesopotamian cities, proving that people were trading with India. More evidence comes from many thousands of clay tablets, which include records of business agreements and complaints about the failure to deliver promised goods.

Silver Boat

The silver model of a boat, found in a royal grave at Ur, tells us two things about Mesopotamian trade. It shows us what ancient boats looked like, and how they were rowed. It is also made of silver, which is not found in Mesopotamia. Look at the map to see where it might have come from.

River Journey

Mesopotamian boats were rowed, using leaf-shaped oars, or punted: pushed along with a pole driven into the river bed. These boats, with both ends curving up to points, are exactly like modern Iraqi river boats. Pictures of boats on seals show that sails were also used for long sea journeys across the Persian Gulf.

At Home

WEBLINK
http://www.odysseyadventures.ca/articles/ur%20of%20the%20chaldees/ur_article.htm#houses

Find out all about the houses of Ur.

Like houses in southern Iraq today, Mesopotamian homes had thick walls of bricks made of mud and chopped straw, dried in the sun. This was the perfect building material to protect the family from the scorching summer heat. Roofs were usually flat, made of palm tree planks with a layer of reed and palm leaf matting, covered with mud.

Courtyard

A woman grinds barley for making bread in the courtyard of her house. This was hard work, which had to be done every day.

Quern

Every home had a quern for grinding barley into flour. The upper stone was pushed backwards and forwards over the grain, lying in the hollow.

HOW DO WE KNOW?

In the 1920s, many houses in Ur, dating from 1900-1740BCE, were excavated by the British archaeologist Leonard Woolley. Scorched walls and ash-covered floors showed that this part of the city had been destroyed by fire. While the dried mud bricks had mostly crumbled away, the lower parts of walls had survived, for these were made of fired brick. The remains of stairs showed that the houses also had upper floors. From all this Woolley worked out the layout of houses.

COURTYARD HOUSE

Here you can see the courtyard of a house in Ur. We know that this is a courtyard rather than an inside room because it has a paved floor which slopes down towards a central drain, to take away rain water. The walls are very thick, to bear the weight of an upper floor.

For security and privacy, Mesopotamian houses rarely had outside windows. Instead, there was often a courtyard, giving light and air to the rooms of the house. Another reason for this arrangement is given by a tablet, which says, "rooms opening out of each other are unlucky, but those opening onto a court bring good luck." The richest people had a central courtyard, with rooms arranged on all four sides, while poorer people might have rooms on just two or three sides, or no courtyard at all. Many of the houses had lavatories, which had paved floors with a hole leading through a pottery drain to a sewer.

A variety of household items have been found, which help us build up a picture of daily life. These include pottery jars, for storing beer and date wine; copper cooking pots; and bowls, plates and cups, made from pottery, stone or copper. Meals were cooked over a fire in the courtyard or in a kitchen. There were also dome-shaped brick ovens, for baking bread.

Tablets from Babylon contain recipes, such as this one for cooking wild hens: "Assemble the following ingredients in a pot with water: a piece of fat … a carefully measured amount of vinegar … pieces of aromatic wood soaked in beer, and rue leaves. When it comes to the boil, add *samidu* (a spicy plant), leek and garlic mashed with onion. Put the birds in this broth and cook."

Temples

Gifts for a God

These worshippers are bringing gifts for their god, which they present to the priests at the entrance to the temple. Gifts include animals and statuettes of worshippers.

Every Mesopotamian city was believed to belong to a main god or goddess, who was worshipped in a great temple in the center of the city. The temple was the home of the god, whose statue was kept there.

As well as being the owner of the city, people believed that each god watched over an aspect of life or nature. Nanna, worshipped in Ur, was the moon god. There were also many lesser gods, who oversaw every possible activity, from brick making to brewing beer.

Ziggurat

From about 2200BCE, tall stepped towers, called ziggurats, were built at the center of each temple. This is the ziggurat of Untash, built between 1265-46BCE by King Untash-Gal of Elam. Like all surviving ziggurats, this one has lost its top. Only three of its five levels still stand.

WORSHIPPER This statuette of a worshipper, his hands clasped in prayer, was presented to the temple of Ninni-Zaza, god of the city of Mari. The statue was supposed to pray to Ninni-Zaza on behalf of the worshipper who presented it. Many statues like this were placed on benches around the inside walls of the temple.

WEBLINK
http://www.crystalinks.com/ziggurat.html

Find out what we know about ziggurats and how they might have been used.

The people of the city visited the temple to ask their gods favors, or to thank them for granting them. They brought with them gifts, such as animals to be sacrificed (killed as offerings to the god). At Ur, merchants returning from long river journeys would present Nanna with a little silver boat, to thank him for protecting them on their journey.

WEBLINK
http://www.mesopotamia.co.uk/gods/challenge/cha_set.html

Take a challenge to match the gods with their cities.

There was a large staff of priests, priestesses and servants who looked after the god's needs. Twice a day, in the morning and evening, the god was given a meal, which was spread on a table before the statue. On special occasions, the statue was taken out of the temple and carried in a procession through the streets. It was sometimes taken to other cities, so that the god could meet other gods. In wartime, the statues accompanied armies into battle. This gave the soldiers the sense that their god was fighting alongside them.

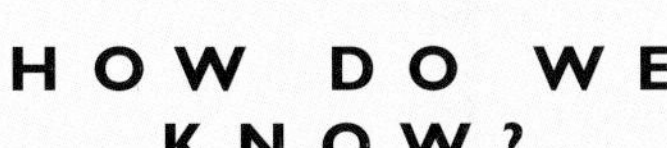

HOW DO WE KNOW?

Around twenty-five ziggurats have been found, some no more than earth mounds. Ancient descriptions help us work out what they looked like. In the fifth century BCE, the Greek writer, Herodotus, visited Babylon and climbed the ziggurat. He said that it had eight levels, with a shelter halfway up, so that people could rest during the climb. On top there was a shrine, in which a bed stood. The Babylonian priests told Herodotus that this was where their god, Bel, slept every night, though Herodotus added, "I do not believe them."

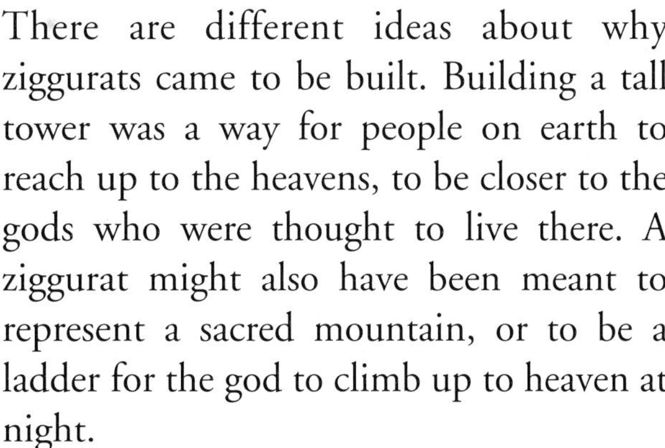

There are different ideas about why ziggurats came to be built. Building a tall tower was a way for people on earth to reach up to the heavens, to be closer to the gods who were thought to live there. A ziggurat might also have been meant to represent a sacred mountain, or to be a ladder for the god to climb up to heaven at night.

In the flat Mesopotamian landscape, ziggurats could be seen for miles around, showing the importance of the gods who lived in them, and the wealth and power of the city which had built them.

Kings

KING
This is how the palace of Ur may have looked in about 2500BCE.
The king, sitting on his throne, is served wine made from dates.
The court is entertained by a female singer and a musician playing a plucked stringed instrument, called a lyre.

FEAST

This is the peace side of the "Standard of Ur," which was perhaps the sounding box of a musical instrument. The figures are made from tiny pieces of shell and red sandstone, while the background is lapis lazuli, a blue stone found in what is now Afghanistan.

While each Sumerian city was thought to belong to a god, it was ruled on the god's behalf by a king. According to Sumerian beliefs, the idea of kingship had come down to earth from heaven at the beginning of time. The king was a chief priest, whose main role was to serve the gods. He built and repaired the city's temples, and played a leading role in religious ceremonies, meant to ensure good harvests. He was also a judge, overseeing law and order, and a war leader, who led his city's army into battle. These roles, of judge and warrior, were also religious. Like kingship, the laws were believed to have come from the gods, and wars were seen as quarrels between rival city gods.

HOW DO WE KNOW?

Sumerian kings wanted people to remember their achievements. So they had their names stamped on the bricks of the temples they built, and they set up inscriptions recording their victories in war. Lists of kings were also preserved, which help us to work out the sequence of rulers in different cities. Evidence of the daily life of courts comes from goods buried in royal graves, including jewellery, lyres, and the "Standard of Ur."

WEBLINK

http://www.wsu.edu:8080/~dee/MESO/GILG.HTM

Find out about Gilgamesh, king of Uruk, the hero of the world's oldest surviving story.

There were a number of different royal titles. A king of a single city was called the *ensi*, which is thought to mean "lord." Through warfare, some kings were able to extend their rule over a number of cities. Their title was *lugal*, which means "big man."

The beautiful box above was discovered in the 1920s by the British archaeologist, Leonard Woolley, in a royal grave at Ur. Unsure of its purpose, Woolley called it the "Standard of Ur." The box has two sides, showing the activities of a king in peace and in war. The peace side depicts a royal feast in the top row. At the top right, you can see a musician playing a lyre and a woman singing. The king, on the left, wears no special royal regalia, such as a crown. However, he can be recognized because he is much bigger than the other figures.

The Great Death Pit

DEATH PIT
One corner of the Death Pit may have looked like this just before the earth was piled on top. The women were all found lying on their sides in neat rows, with their legs slightly bent as if they were asleep. Beside each of them was a bowl made of stone or metal.

In 1928-9, the British archaeologist, Leonard Woolley made an amazing discovery while digging in the ancient city of Ur. He found a deep rectangular pit, dating from about 2700-2400BCE, in which sixty-eight women lay buried. By the entrance to the pit, approached by a ramp, six men's bodies lay in a line, as if on guard. This mass grave also contained four lyres and two beautiful statuettes of male goats. Woolley called his discovery "the Great Death Pit." Like a detective, he tried to solve the mystery of the burial. How had they died, and why had they been buried with such beautiful treasures?

LYRE
This is one of four lyres discovered in the pit. It was made of wood completely covered in silver, and was decorated with a silver cow's head with eyes of lapis lazuli and shell. Although the wood had rotted away, the silver covering allowed the lyre to be restored.

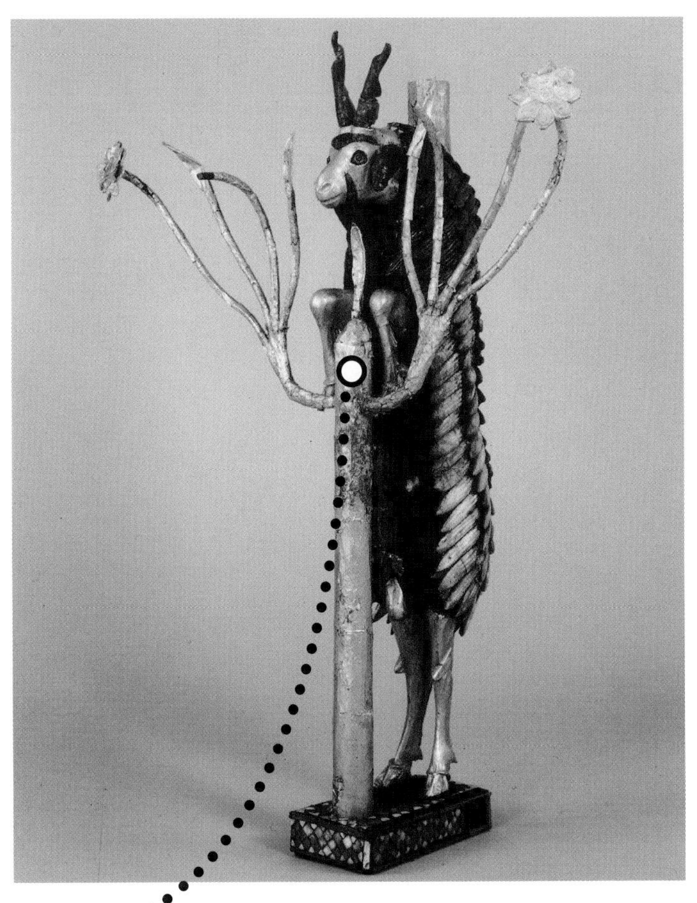

Woolley had already uncovered many Mesopotamian graves, and was used to finding goods buried with the dead. In most cases, bodies were wrapped in a reed mat and placed in the earth with pots, beads and tools. This was evidence that people believed in a life after death, a next world where they could take their belongings with them. From writings, we know that they called this world "the land of no return."

GOLDEN GOAT

In one corner of the pit, Woolley found this statuette of a male goat. It stands on its hind legs, reaching up to eat the golden leaves of a tree. Its legs and face are covered in gold, while its fleece is made from lapis lazuli and shell. Like the lyre, it was carefully restored after it was discovered.

The Death Pit was one of sixteen graves in Ur in which groups of people had been buried with rich treasures, including the "Standard of Ur," shown on pages 19 and 22. Woolley believed that these were royal graves, and that the people were attendants or courtiers, who had been chosen to accompany their king or queen to the next world.

Because there were no obvious signs of violence, Woolley suggested that the men and women had entered it of their own free will. They had then drunk poison or a sleeping drug from the bowls which lay beside them, before the earth was piled on top.

WEBLINK

http://www.mesopotamia.co.uk/tombs/explore/exp_main.html#plan_top

Explore for yourself the tombs Woolley found at Ur.

HOW DO WE KNOW?

Although Woolley's theory explains what might have happened, we will never know for certain if it is true. The bodies were too badly decayed to tell how or when they died. Other theories have been suggested. One idea is that the women were priestesses, who were sacrificed as an offering to the gods. Another is that they were people who were already dead, and whose bodies had been stored elsewhere in order to be finally buried beside their king or queen. The mystery of the Great Death Pit remains.

Warfare

In Sumer, there were a dozen separate city states, which often quarrelled with each other over farm land or the water supply. These quarrels often led to warfare. Each of the cities was surrounded by a strong brick wall, needed for protection from other cities and also foreign invaders.

The first recorded war took place in about 2500BCE, between the cities of Lagash and Umma. Eannatum, king of Lagash, won the war and then had a stele, or upright stone, set up, celebrating his victory. It shows his army on the march, while his dead enemies are being eaten by vultures. Another victorious Sumerian army, from about the same time, is shown below, on the "Standard of Ur."

WEBLINK
http://joseph_berrigan.tripod.com/ancientbabylon/id46.html

Find out about warfare among the early Sumerians.

In an inscription of about 2050BCE, Shulgi, king of Ur, boasted of his skill at winning battles, which he claimed to fight on behalf of his god, Enlil: "When I set off for battle to a place that Enlil has commanded me, I go ahead of my troops. I have a passion for weapons. Not only do I carry my spear and lance, I also know how to handle a sling. The clay pellets that I shoot fly around like a violent rainstorm. In my rage I do not let them miss."

STANDARD OF UR
The war side of the Standard of Ur (see page 19) shows four-wheeled chariots, pulled by onagers (wild asses), and soldiers armed with spears and axes. In the top row, soldiers bring prisoners to the king, who has just stepped down from his chariot.

INTO BATTLE
Sumerian soldiers marched in tight ranks, protected by long shields, probably made of leather on wooden frames. They carried bronze pointed spears and wore copper helmets. The king and his leading men rode chariots into battle.

We can also read laments, poems of sorrow, which show us the viewpoint of the defeated. This lament was written after Ur was destroyed by the Elamites, in 2000BCE: "Ur is destroyed, bitter is its lament. The country's blood now fills its holes like hot bronze in a mould... Our temple is destroyed, the gods have abandoned us...."

HOW DO WE KNOW?

As well as the victory stele (see page 22) and the "Standard of Ur," archaeologists have found much evidence for early Mesopotamian warfare. The soldiers buried in the Death Pit at Ur wore copper helmets, just like those shown on the standard. Weapons including bronze axes, spears and swords have also been discovered. Digging at Ur, Leonard Woolley found that large areas of the city were blackened by fire, evidence of Ur's second destruction, by the Babylonians, in 1738BCE.

The King's Laws

RIVER TRIAL
This woman is being thrown into the River Euphrates, as a trial by ordeal, a type of test. If she survives, she will be declared innocent and freed. If she drowns, it will be a sign that the gods have judged her guilty and punished her. King Hammurabi watches from the river bank.

King and God
On top of the stele of Hammurabi is a carving of the king standing before Shamash, god of justice and the sun, identified by flames rising from his shoulders. The picture was meant to show that the king was making laws on behalf of the god of justice.

One of the most important duties of a Mesopotamian king was to oversee justice. Kings had to give decisions in quarrels over land or property, and they tried and punished criminals. They also wrote the first laws, in which they listed punishments for various crimes, and described how cases should be judged. The most complete early law list is that of King Hammurabi, ruler of Babylon from 1792-50BCE. He had his laws carved on a 7 1/2 foot high cone-shaped stele.

WEBLINK
http://eawc.evansville.edu/anthology/hammurabi.htm

Read all the laws of Hammurabi.

Hammurabi's stele has forty-nine columns in which 282 laws are listed. Among them, a son who struck his father would have both his hands chopped off. A man who put out the eye of another man would have his own eye put out. Most of these laws were not invented by Hammurabi, but were based on existing customs. The stele describes a "river ordeal," shown in the picture on the left, used when it was not clear if someone accused of a serious crime was guilty or innocent. This ordeal is also described in the oldest known law code, written three hundred years before Hammurabi's time, by a king of Ur.

At the end of the list, Hammurabi explained that he had set the stele up as an example to later rulers: "To the end of days, forever, may the king who happens to be in the land observe the words of justice which I have inscribed on my stele… let that stele reveal to him the accustomed way, the way to follow, the land's judgements which I have judged."

HOW DO WE KNOW?

The stele of Hammurabi was discovered in the winter of 1901, by the French archaeologist, Jean-Vincent Scheil. He found it not in Babylon, where Hammurabi had set it up, but in Susa, capital of Elam, in present-day Iran. In 1165BCE, the Elamites attacked Babylon and took the stele away with them as booty. When Scheil found the stele, it was broken into three pieces. He put them back together, and then spent six months translating the writing. Today, you can see Hammurabi's stele in the Louvre Museum in Paris.

Empire

The most warlike Mesopotamian people were the Assyrians, who lived in the northern cities of Ashur, Ninevah, Nimrud and Khorsabad. Between 950 and 612BCE, the Assyrians conquered an empire which stretched across the Middle East, from western Persia (now Iran) to northern Egypt.

The wealth of the Assyrian Empire allowed kings to build some of the biggest palaces found in Mesopotamia. Palace walls were covered in painted stone reliefs showing kings worshipping gods, hunting lions, and leading the Assyrian army into battle. The aim was to impress any visitor to the palace with the power of the Assyrian king.

WINGED BULL
This great winged bull with a human head stood guard by a doorway in the palace of King Sargon II in Khorsabad. Similar winged bulls and lions have been found in several Assyrian palaces.

SARGON
King Sargon II, who ruled the Assyrian Empire from 721-705BCE, leads a procession through his vast palace at Khorsabad.

WEBLINK

http://www.mesopotamia.co.uk/palaces/home_set.html

http://www.mesopotamia.co.uk/warfare/index.html

Find out about the palaces of Assyria and Assyrian warfare.

ATTACK
This wall carving of Assyrian soldiers attacking a city was found in the palace of King Tiglath-piliser III in Nimrud. At the bottom, enemy heads are chopped off. In one palace inscription, an Assyrian king boasted, "I cut off their heads and piled them up at the walls of their cities like heaps of grain."

By the first millennium BCE, many new ways of fighting had been invented. Bronze weapons had been replaced by iron ones, which were harder and sharper-edged. The Assyrians also used horses, which they rode and used to pull fast two-wheeled chariots. They were expert at capturing walled cities, using great battering rams and siege towers. They were also extremely cruel. Wall carvings in Assyrian palaces show defeated enemies being skinned alive, while palace inscriptions left by kings boast of their cruelty: "I built a pillar over against his city gate and I skinned all the chief men … and I covered the pillar with their skins. Some I walled up within the pillar, some I impaled upon the pillar on stakes."

HOW DO WE KNOW?

Unlike earlier Mesopotamian peoples, such as the Sumerians, the Assyrians were never forgotten. The Bible describes their destruction of the kingdom of Israel, when they carried off ten Jewish tribes, who were never heard from again. Between CE1842-55, an Englishman, Austen Henry Layard, and a Frenchman, Paul-Emile Botta, rediscovered the Assyrian cities, in what is now northern Iraq. They uncovered palace wall carvings, showing the army on campaign, and found Assyrian accounts which backed up the Biblical story of the destruction of Israel.

Eventually, the cruelty of the Assyrians led to widespread rebellions. The king of Babylon joined forces with the Medes, (who lived to the east of Mesopotamia), and destroyed the empire. In 614-612BCE, the Assyrian cities were burned to the ground.

Timeline

A NOTE ABOUT DATES

All the dates in this timeline are BCE dates. This stands for "before the Common Era." BCE dates are counted back from the year 1, which is taken to be the beginning of the Common Era (CE). There was no year 0. These dates work in the same way as BC (before Christ) and AD (*Anno Domini*, which means "the year of our Lord").

Some dates have the letter "c." in front of them. This stands for *circa*, which means "around." These dates are guesses, because no one knows what the real date is.

c. 5000BCE Farmers from northern Mesopotamia move into the flat southern plains.

c. 4000-3500BCE Villages at Ur, Uruk and other southern sites grow into towns.

c. 3500-2800BCE The towns grow into cities. Large temples are built.

c. 3100BCE Earliest known use of cuneiform writing, in Uruk.

c. 3000BCE Bronze used for tools and weapons. Four wheeled chariot used in war.

c. 2750-2400BCE First dynasty of Ur. Kings and queens of Ur are buried in rich mass graves.

c. 2500BCE Earliest recorded war, between Lagash and Umma.

c. 2330BCE Sargon of Akkad conquers all of Sumer.

c. 2220BCE The Gutians from Gutiam in the eastern mountains conquer Akkad and Sumer.

c. 2113-2096BCE Reign of Ur-Nammu, founder of the third dynasty of Ur, who throws off Gutian rule.

c. 2095-47BCE Reign of Shulgi of Ur, who builds the great ziggurat.

c. 2000BCE The Elamites (from Elam in the east) destroy Ur and capture the king.

c. 1900BCE The Amorites (people from the western deserts) conquer much of Mesopotamia, ruling from Babylon.

1792-50BCE Reign of King Hammurabi of Babylon, who rules over Akkad and Sumer, now called Babylonia, and part of Assyria.

1738BCE Ur destroyed again, by the Babylonians.

c. 1600BCE Two foreign peoples, the Hittites and Kassites, invade Mesopotamia.

Iron weapons and fast chariots pulled by horses now used in war.

c. 1570BCE Kassite kings rule Babylon. Their dynasty rules for almost 500 years.

c. 950BCE Assyrians begin to conquer their empire.

612BCE Fall of the Assyrian Empire, replaced by the Babylonian Empire.

605-562BCE Reign of Nebuchadrezzar II of Babylon, who conquers Syria and Palestine, destroys Jerusalem and takes the Jews as captives to Babylon.

539BCE Cyrus the Great of Persia conquers Babylonian Empire.

331BCE Alexander the Great of Macedon (to the north of ancient Greece) conquers the Persian Empire. He makes Babylon his capital.

c. CE75 Last use of cuneiform script.

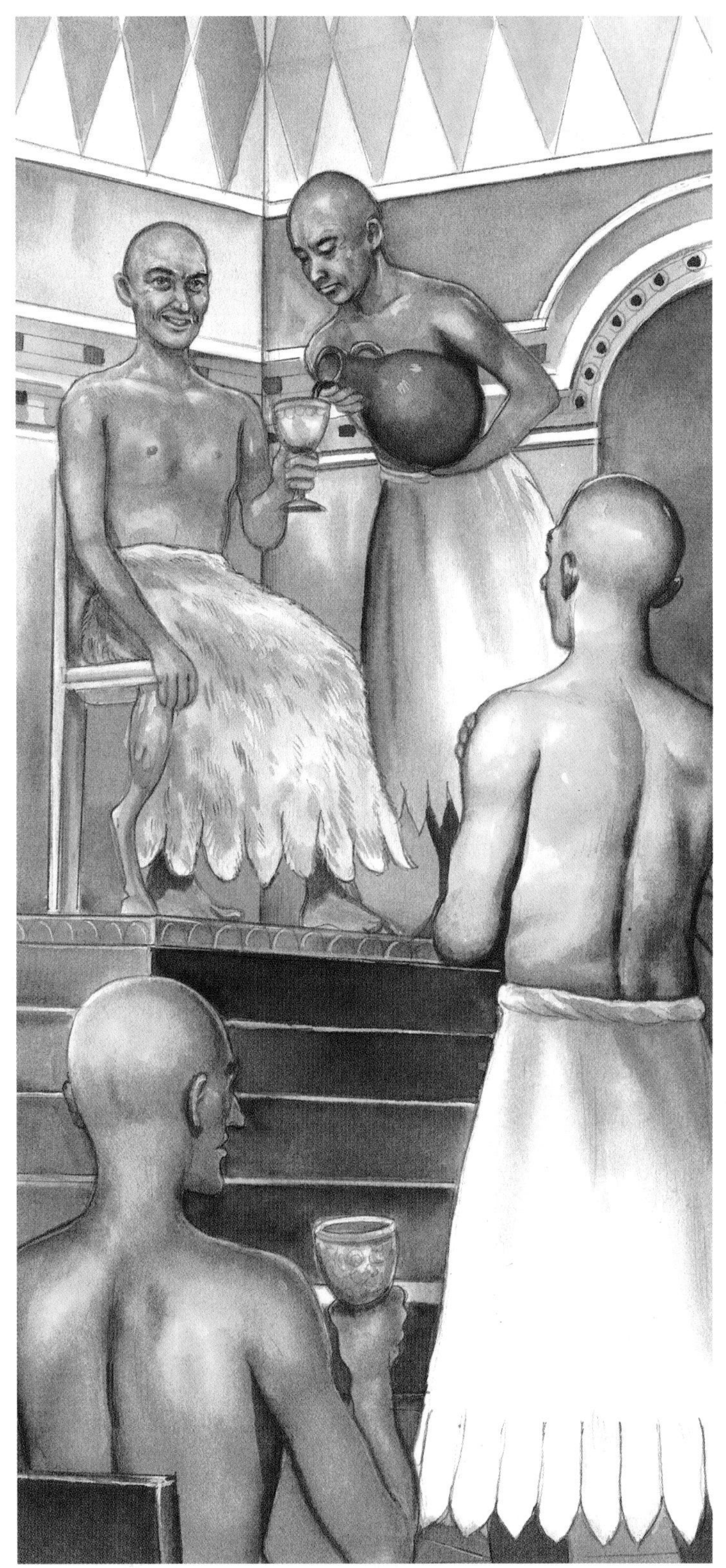

Glossary

Akkad Central region of Mesopotamia, where the Tigris and Euphrates come closest together.

Akkadian The name given to the people from Akkad, and also the language spoken in Akkad.

Archaeologist A person who finds out about the past by looking for the remains of buildings and other objects, often beneath the ground and studying them.

Assyria Northern region of Mesopotamia, based on the cities of Ashur, Ninevah, Nimrud and Khorsabad.

Babylonia The name given to Sumer and Akkad after they were united under the rule of the kings of Babylon.

BCE Used in dates. Means "before the Common Era."

Bitumen Natural tar, which seeps out of the ground.

Carnelian Precious red stone found in India, also spelled cornelian.

CE Used in dates. Means "the Common Era." The common Era begins with year 1 which is the same as the year AD1 in the Christian calendar.

Cuneiform Writing system used in Mesopotamia. The name means "wedge shaped."

Cylinder seal A roller-shaped piece of stone, shell or metal, carved with pictures and writing, pressed into clay or wax to sign letters and seal containers or doors.

Date A sweet, dark brown, oval fruit which grows on a tall palm tree.

Dynasty A family line of kings.

Elam Country to the east of Sumer, with a capital at Susa, in present day Iran.

Elamite The name given to the people from Elam, and also the language spoken in Elam.

Fertile crescent Semi-circular region stretching from the Mediterranean to the Persian Gulf, where farming was first practiced. "Fertile" means able to produce new life.

Indus Civilization Early Indian civilization, lasting from 3100-1700 BC, based on cities around the River Indus in northern India.

Irrigation The control of water for the purposes of farming. An example is the digging of a canal or ditch, to take water from a river to a field.

Lapis lazuli A bright blue stone used in jewellery and sculptures.

Mesopotamia The Greek name for the land between the Tigris and the Euphrates rivers. It means "between the rivers."

Onager A wild ass.

Persia The region to the east of Mesopotamia, now called Iran.

Pollination To sprinkle pollen on a flower, so that it can produce fruit.

Reservoir A specially built place for storing water.

Sacrifice Killing an animal as an offering to a god.

Scribe A person who writes or keeps records.

Further information

Sewer An underground pipe or channel for carrying away waste and water.

Shrine A building housing something holy, such as the statue of a god.

Siege When an army surrounds a town or a building and cuts off its supplies, in order to force the people inside to surrender.

Silt Fine soil carried by water.

Stele Upright stone or pillar carved with an inscription or picture, usually on behalf of a ruler.

Stylus Pointed instrument, such as a cut reed, used for writing on clay or wax.

Sumer The southern region of Mesopotamia, where the first cities such as Ur and Uruk were built.

Sumerian The name given to the people from Sumer, and also the language spoken in Sumer.

Tablet A small flat piece of clay, used for writing on.

Tell An Arabic word for a mound. Tells are made of fallen walls, pottery, stones and other debris left behind by ancient settlements.

Ziggurat A tall temple tower resembling a pyramid, but built in stepped stages with a shrine on top.

Books to Read

The City of Rainbows: A Tale from Ancient Sumer by Karen Foster (University of Pennsylvania Museum Publications, 1999)

Find out about Mesopotamia: What Life Was Like in Ancient Sumer, Babylon and Assyria by Lorna Oakes (Southwater, 2003)

First Civilizations (Cultural Atlas for Young People) by Erica C. D. Hunter, (Facts on File Ltd, 1994)

First Civilizations: From 10,000BC to 1500BC by Anne Millard (Usborne Publishing Ltd, 1992)

Looking Back: Mesopotamia and the Near East: From 10,000BC to 539BC by John Malam (Evans Brothers, 1999)

CD-ROM

Atlas of the Ancient World (Maris Multimedia Ltd, 1997)

Index